HISTORIC SCOTLAND

Historic Scotland preserves and maintains a major part of Scotland's rich built heritage and some of the finest properties under its care are pictured here.

Many are worth visiting for their magnificent settings alone, doubly so for the glimpses of the past they offer. It is hoped that these photographs will be enjoyed by visitor and resident alike, inspiring further explorations of the sites and buildings and the rich cultural variety of Scotland's historic and industrial past.

EDINBURGH : HMSO

HISTORIC SCOTLAND

Top Crimson velvet and ermine cushion the priceless stones of Scotland's Crown.

Bottom *The Edinburgh Evening Courant* in 1819 carries news that the Regalia of Scotland will be available for (limited) public inspection.

Opposite Edinburgh, this most famous of Scottish castles as seen from the fountain in Princes Street Gardens.

HISTORIC SCOTLAND

HISTORIC SCOTLAND

Opposite The Stones of Stenness cast sharp shadows in the Orkney morning.

Top The remarkable Standing Stones of Callanish, on Lewis, at the westernmost edge of the Western Isles.

Bottom A stone at Orkney's magical Neolithic Ring of Brodgar stands tall against the setting sun.

HISTORIC SCOTLAND

Left One of the magnificent collection of Pictish stones at Meigle Museum in Tayside.

Right Beautiful and intricate sculpture from the Dark Ages on another Meigle stone.

Opposite Mysterious Pictish symbols decorate this sculptured stone at Aberlemno in Tayside.

HISTORIC SCOTLAND

HISTORIC SCOTLAND

Opposite Inhabited from the Bronze Age to the seventeenth century, the important complex at Jarlshof, on Shetland, reveals some of its secrets.

Top A sylvan setting at Glenelg, near Kyle of Lochalsh, for one of the sturdy brochs that sheltered the region's prehistoric inhabitants.

Bottom A stone doorway frames a stone hearth in Western Europe's best preserved group of Stone-Age houses, at Skara Brae on Orkney.

HISTORIC SCOTLAND

Top A medieval stonemason's work at Melrose Abbey portrays a face and expression recognisable today.

Bottom A smiling face to greet the visitor at Arbroath Abbey.

Opposite Expressive and delicate stonecarving at Dryburgh Abbey in the Borders.

HISTORIC SCOTLAND

HISTORIC SCOTLAND

Opposite This elegant archway leads into the remains of the lovely late thirteenth-century cathedral at Elgin, in Moray.

Top A solid Romanesque archway adorns the great Benedictine abbey at Dunfermline.

Bottom Flying buttresses form a tunnel at Linlithgow Palace.

HISTORIC SCOTLAND

Top Glasgow Cathedral (St. Mungo's) is the only Scottish mainland medieval cathedral to have survived the Reformation complete.

Bottom The remains of Scotland's largest cathedral at St. Andrews. The cathedral museum houses an outstanding collection of Christian monuments found at the site.

Opposite In St. Margaret's Chapel in Edinburgh Castle the colours of this stained glass window of St. Margaret herself startle with their brilliance.

HISTORIC SCOTLAND

Left Sixteenth-century carved timber panel from the Abbot's House at Arbroath Abbey.

Top right A bronze dragonesque brooch, found recently in Iron-Age levels at Edinburgh Castle.

Bottom left The intricate carving on the early twelfth-century ivory Jedburgh comb.

Opposite The splendid nave in Dunfermline's twelfth-century abbey.

HISTORIC SCOTLAND

HISTORIC SCOTLAND

Opposite The finely-made arcade in the cloister of the elegant ruins of Melrose Abbey.

Top Romantic Dryburgh Abbey makes a fitting burial place for Sir Walter Scott.

Bottom The detailed carving of Dryburgh Abbey, just as romantic by day.

HISTORIC SCOTLAND

Rounded posies of flowers growing in the square recesses of
Edzell Castle's seventeenth-century walled garden in Tayside.

HISTORIC SCOTLAND

Top Military precision is suggested in the sharp angles of the star-shaped fortification of Corgarff Castle in Grampian, converted from a tower house to Hanoverian barracks in 1748.

Bottom A sixteenth-century 'beehive' doocot nestles in the grounds of Dirleton Castle in East Lothian.

HISTORIC SCOTLAND

Top The moated castle of Caerlaverock in Dumfries and Galloway—one of the finest of Scotland's many castles.

Bottom The massive front of the fourteenth-century Doune Castle in Perthshire, set on a carpet of flowers.

HISTORIC SCOTLAND

Top Fast on its island stands forbidding Threave Castle in Dumfries and Galloway, built in the late fourteenth century by Archibald the Grim, 3rd Earl of Black Douglas.

Bottom Tantallon Castle, on its rocky perch, stands guard over the Firth of Forth, as it has done for more than six centuries.

HISTORIC SCOTLAND

The insignia for the four Orders of Chivalry
decorate the outer entry of Linlithgow Palace, where
Mary Queen of Scots was born.

Opposite The island fortress of Lochleven, where Queen Mary
was imprisoned for almost a year.

HISTORIC SCOTLAND

Left The brilliant military strategist and patriotic Scot Sir William Wallace occupies a niche in the gatehouse of Edinburgh Castle.

Right Stirling Castle's statue of one of Scotland's greatest heroes, Robert the Bruce, King Robert I of Scotland, the victor of Bannockburn.

Opposite High above the town of Stirling, on a rocky outcrop, stands the castle, commanding and impressive in its grandeur.

HISTORIC SCOTLAND

HISTORIC SCOTLAND

Carefully renovated, and in full working order, the water-powered New Abbey Corn Mill in Dumfries and Galloway.

HISTORIC SCOTLAND

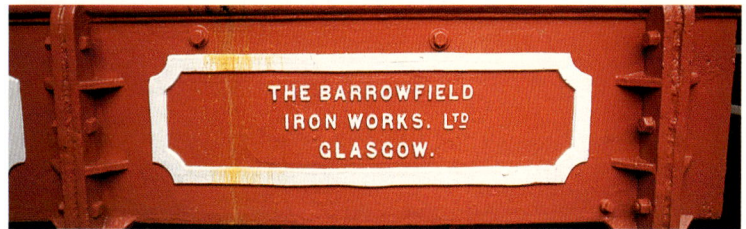

Top High over the Tweed Valley near Melrose, Leaderfoot viaduct's Victorian stonework glows warm against scattering of winter snow.

Bottom A monument to Scotland's industrial past – a maker's nameplate in Biggar Gasworks, the only surviving small town coal-gas works in Scotland.

HISTORIC SCOTLAND

Opposite Take time to see how fine malt whisky used to be made at the Dallas Dhu Distillery near Forres in Grampian.

Top A tempting barrel of Dallas Dhu malt whisky.

Bottom A very fine old label from a bottle of fine old malt.

Photography: Historic Scotland Picture Library
Front Cover: Linlithgow Palace and Loch
Back Cover: The Royal Arms of Scotland emblazoned on the Portcullis Gate in Edinburgh Castle
End papers: Floor tiles from the medieval abbey at Melrose in the Borders.

© Crown copyright 1994

First published 1994

Application for reproduction should be made to HMSO

British Library Cataloguing in Publication Data

A catalogue record for this book is available from the British Library

Designed by Graham Galloway

HMSO Graphic Design Edinburgh

ISBN 0 11 495204 3

HMSO publications are available from:

HMSO Publications Centre
(Mail, fax and telephone orders only)
PO Box 276, London, SW8 5DT
Telephone orders 071-873 9090
General enquiries 071-873 0011
(queuing system in operation for both numbers)
Fax orders 071-873 8200

HMSO Bookshops
71 Lothian Road, Edinburgh, EH3 9AZ
031-228 4181 Fax 031-229 2734
49 High Holborn, London, WC1V 6HB
071-873 0011 Fax 071-873 8200 (counter service only)
258 Broad Street, Birmingham, B1 2HE
021-643 3740 Fax 021-643 6510
33 Wine Street, Bristol, BS1 2BQ
0272 264306 Fax 0272 294515
9-21 Princess Street, Manchester, M60 8AS
061-834 7201 Fax 061-833 0634
16 Arthur Street, Belfast, BT1 4GD
0232 238451 Fax 0232 235401

HMSO's Accredited Agents
(see Yellow Pages)

and through good booksellers